WILL TURN HELL INTO PARADISE

Just Wait!

WILL TURN HELL INTO PARADISE

Just Wait!

Poems Translated from Malayalam

Akbar

EXCELLER BOOKS®
A GLOBAL PRESS

Will Turn Hell into Paradise
Just Wait!

Cover by Exceller Books using resources from Pixabay.com

ISBN: 978-93-48892-26-3

First published in India in 2025 by Exceller Books,
An imprint of GE Group
G1, Dream Apartment, Degree College Road, Belgharia,
Kolkata, 700056, India
www.excellerbooks.com

EXCELLER BOOKS®
A GLOBAL PRESS

Acknowledgement

I express my deepest gratitude to my parents, who, despite their struggles with illiteracy and poverty, have wholeheartedly supported my journey as a writer. The lush greenery of Neriamangalam village played a profound role in shaping my creative path—its forests and rivers gently steering me from my childhood dream of painting towards the world of poetry. I am also immensely thankful to my teachers and friends for their encouragement and guidance. However, above all, it is my village that has been my greatest source of inspiration.

The Wild Paths of Poetry

Have you ever seen a path in the forest? You can never say where it ends, for often, it halts before a sprawling swamp or stumbles and fades among the trees. That is how poetry feels to me—quickly fading, leaving me restless and wandering back and forth, unsure of what to do next. Once, in the Thattekad forest on Environment Day, I stood there just like that—lost, unsure of the path. But then, the sun between the leaves showed me the direction. Writing, for me, is like entering those forest paths.

Poetry guided me during my college days in Kothamangalam. Before that, painting was my preference. Somehow, that path led me to writing, and over time, I met friends who shared this journey. I believe my own struggle lies in how life inevitably intertwines with my poetry. Like I mentioned before, poetry feels like a restless pause along a forest path—maybe a result of a life shaped since childhood; I'm not sure.

In this poetic journey of two decades, I hold no grievances against anyone. But, like rain cascading down from the mountains, drumming over the river like the beat of a tabla, there is, at times, a feeling of unease—the worry that the home might get soaked and damaged. Yet, that feeling fades away, just as my Umma lovingly cleans the mud-splattered floor after the rain.

As the only child in a family with illiterate parents, I feel that the solitude I've experienced since childhood may be what shapes my poetry. Neriamangalam, the forests, and the river frequently appear in it, though it's not an anti-human view of the environment. I'm simply marking the places I've lived.

Moreover, this book contains various kinds of poems, each carrying some of my own experiences.

I think I try to bring forth strange dreams, political ideas, and protests through my poetry. That's the nature of the poems in this collection. Many of them were written unknowingly, almost as if they sprouted naturally, like the greenery of my native land. I am constantly trying to bring changes to it, like sunlight spreading over the hills, only for the rain to come and wash it away. I write in this quiet way—nothing more.

Here is a set of poems that moves the reader deeply with hope and pain. They are intimate, emotional, and well-crafted. Akbar has genuine poetry in him and I have no doubt he will soon find a respectable place among the Malayalam poets available in English, who, unfortunately, are too few.

Akbar,
Poet

Discovering the Transformation of Malayalam Poetry through Akbar

While reading contemporary Malayalam poet Akbar's poem in English, I could realize the transformation in Malayalam poetry. I have translated from Balamaniyamma to Ayyappa Panikker and more, so my image of Malayalam poetry was different. Akbar's poetry is simpler and communicates very well with the contemporary world, making it more universal. What I like most is the simplicity of expression in these poems. A positive attitude is another quality of these poems. When there is a fear of the next world war, Akbar says—"Will turn hell into paradise, just wait!" He wishes—"Life silent like love and detached like God."

It is not that he is unaffected by war. He says—

"I remember the children/of Ukraine/Palestine, Yazidi/Israel/and Somalia.../all fell to their deaths before my eyes."

A poet cannot and should not support any side in a war; that is why he remembers the children of Israel as well. Most of the time, we become emotional and forget about the children on the enemy's side. I always say that in any war, women and children suffer on both sides.

Akbar's love poems are very soft and emotional. He says—"I offered a glass of rain /to start the conversation/but she wanted warmth./After having something sweet,/she continued staring at the corner of the room."

In this cruel time, we are forgetting love or the softness of love. Modern love poems are losing that softness. *Silence at a Crescendo* impressed me as a very soft, feminine poem, which shows the sensitive nature of the poet.

“There are some feminine dreams/Where only silence reigns./One should rush in and rush off/After planting a kiss./The lips and cheeks would bloom/Like flowers scented with/Sudden exclamations.”

The poet knows how an erotic expression can be soft and beautiful.

"Will turn hell into paradise, just wait!" is a very interesting poem. This is a direct conversation with God—
“O my Creator,/I want to sprawl/As a white sheet of paper/From which poetry has drained away. Sprawled on my back/Covered in a coarse white cotton sheet.”
The best thing about these poems is their language, which is simple and beautiful. Credit also goes to the translator. But I am sure they are beautiful in Malayalam as well. Another good thing is that they communicate with the poet directly.

These poems are more open to world readers. However, I think he should write poems related to his land, language, and society. Since I have read only the translated poems, it is possible that he has traditional poems as well.

My congratulations to the poet and the translator for bringing out a beautiful book for non-Malayalam readers.

Rati Saxena,
Poet

Contents

In Wait

Translated by Devi Priya

As those who were expected
Didn't reach,
Staying in wait
For the expected to arrive.

Will Turn Hell into Paradise, Just Wait!

Translated by Ra Sh

O my Creator,
I want to sprawl
As a white sheet of paper
From which poetry has drained away.
Sprawled on my back
Covered in a coarse white cotton sheet.

When the angels come to interrogate
I can tell a lie that
I skipped the classes in this world.
I can bicker that I will write the supplementary.

Yet,
If you dump me in some hell
Upon God
Upon you
I will form a gang of robbers.

I will rob the heavens
Without the angels knowing.
I will channelize
The rivers of honey to hell.
Will kidnap the houries
And make them dance topless.

I will bit into a pipe
And order around in English
Not in Arabic.
The angels who do not follow English
May break into a sweat...ha...ha!

I will make Lucifer wear
A striped vest
And make him pay obeisance.

With the wealth
Robbed from the heaven
I will turn hell into a paradise.
At the edges of hell, I will plant
Rehaan plants.

After that,
I want to lie down sprawled
On a white sheet of poetry.
Want to hide myself
Among the leaves of wild poetry.

Come, my Creator,
Let's play hide and seek.

Milchama*

Translated by Arun T. Vijayan

Do you remember?
We were the house mates,
Sharing the same room.
We cooked and served ourselves
The pieces of happiness and sorrows.
We argued about football and tennis,
Spent time watching TV
And reading books together.
We fought and stayed silent.
We embraced and lost ourselves.
'Bicycle Thieves'* was the movie you liked,
While for me, it was 'Children of Heaven.'*
That must be why
You loved bicycles.
How could I forget
You riding them?

Now, we're not in the same room,
Not in the same house,
And not even in the same country.

When I watch the news,
I always remember you.
You must be hiding among the tankers.

Even so,
Will we ever speak together again—
In this same house, in this same room?

The sky is full of fighter jets,

Flapping their wings in the gray hue.
I move on to the bunker
After extinguishing the memory of
A loud noise that pierced my mind.

You may come back some day!
I'm waiting for you with
'Shalom Aleichem'* on my lips.
Please say 'As-Salamu Alaikum'*
When you see me.

We need to fight and gather together,
And then run among the date palms and olives,
Touching their leaves.
We need to recite and pray
The Torah and Quran in the moonlight.

Hopefully, at least then,
There will be a clear sky and beautiful nightlight.

---

*Milchama–the Hebrew word referring to war and peace
*Bicycle Thieves–Italian movie
*Children of Heaven–Iranian movie
*Shalom Aleichem–"Peace be upon you." It is often used as a warm and friendly greeting, particularly in Jewish communities.
*As-Salamu Alaikum – "Peace be upon you." It is commonly used among Muslims as a way to greet one another and convey wishes for peace. The typical response is "Wa Alaikum As-Salam," which means "And upon you be peace."

War Game

Translated by Arun T. Vijayan

In the morning,
I Dreamed
That all the children in the world
Had Fallen to their deaths.
All the jasmine in my courtyard
Bloomed Without fragrance.
I Rubbed my weary eyes,
Peeked Into my children's room—
But They were not there.
I Try to recall the dream I had,
The Memory of children playing
Amidst Wars returns to me.
And The fireballs falling upon them
Still Weigh heavily on my mind.
My Words,
Once Running with a cry,
Are Now fading away.
I Remember the children
Of Ukraine,
Palestine,
Yazidi,
Israel,
And Somalia...
All Fell to their deaths before my eyes.
I Searched for my children
Through Rooms and yards,
Fear Rising within me.
Their Smiling faces
Suddenly Turned
To Bloodstained memories.

My Phone rang,
I Answered, heavy with dread.
Vaappee*...
We're Here playing war.
When I asked where,
They Said,
In The world of children—
And Hung up the phone.
Yes,
In The world of children,
There Are no problems, are there?
With A cannon in hand,
I Aimed toward the neighbor's yard
And Pulled the trigger...
The Jasmine flowers
Fell To the ground.

---

*Vappee: A term used by Kerala Muslims to refer to 'father'.

Hosanna

Translated by Arun T. Vijayan

At dawn's zenith,
A tender palm frond
Sways to the tolling
Church bells.

In Jerusalem,
Olive branches flutter
Over wounded children.

Where is the Messiah?
Bombs echo with
Wails of sorrow.

In the streets, grief
Has spread itself out,
Alongside prayers.

Black Sun

Translated by Binu Karunakaran

Rising Sun takes
Long strides running
Into daybreak
Skipping the rattan
Mat spread on courtyard.
Future Dawns are terrific
Not ones that have passed,
Loudly state the people
As they walk past.
All movements now
Have been neatly fenced.
No distances, only intimacies
It chants climbing
Atop the new day's shoulder.
Would there be others
Beyond the fences?
Would they all have names?
Through the fence
A sapling's head appears
It has no documents,
Bounding lines vanish
As tree limbs reach
Out to caress. Here
The night lies down
Resting its head.
Darkness begins to knead
The black needed for
The next day's sun.

Solitude of Love

Translated by Haris Yoonus

Somewhere in a village
Full of multi-coloured trees and houses,
Your home exists.
How vibrant I am
To meet you!
I laundered the past days to fresh,
Just formed new one
And woke up to the dawn of that day.
Ahead of coconut trees awakening,
Not to have woken up the birds and beetles,
Gathered the jars with tranquillity
Without seeping a bit..
The tongue stands still,
Noises surrounding me
Faded at once.
A shirt woven with nights' yellowish moonbeam,
Jasmines embedded dhoti,
White pollen smeared on the face,
Washing my hands in the stream,
Head straight and hair neatly combed,
Wearing fragrance of mist
Under the arms and ears.
In the yard, the plants lay with their leaves folded,
And the fields ahead stretched without a single tremor.
Your home stands on a hill
Among the mountains.
Perhaps, since you live there,
It is prettier than the rest!
Isn't it due to you,

That even the world itself smiles
With such stillness?
In my pocket, I keep poems for you,
Poems never borne before.
With the love of poems,
My pocket fills with glow.
Noises stored in the jars
Begin to hum,
And trees and plants
Sing along.
Not loud though,
Softly,
Softer than a river on the edge of the woods.
Walking uphill and down,
I reach close to your home.
Roses in your courtyard
Bloom at once,
Light cascades from the coconut trees,
And the river at the valley
Flows blue...
Instantly
Instantly...
Everyone but you fade away from the house.
Now, only you remain!
In that light, even the sun
Meant to rise hours later, trembles.
The moon, until now steadfast,
Melts into the river.
Just you and the house,
And you without the house.
And at that moment,
When did I become you?

A flutter to the dawn,
I flew away.
Might I find your form in the birds close by?
The world however
Knew none of this!
Love was left alone.
The world turned crimson
With screams.

In Memories

Translated by Ra Sh

He loved
Moonlit nights reeking of illicit brews
And places where the rain fell thick and fat
And the jungles and the rivers.

He, who did not relish
Reveries or words about women.

Boys were spied
Walking with him joyfully.
Like balloons soaring away.

Trees with smoke swirling around
Their tops till they drooped down.

He sketched flowers on my thighs
In the shade of the woods
After the rains.
Spring blossomed on the loins.

Each flower reminds me now
Of the way the forest lay supine
And, the way he lay.

Wandering

Translated by Achuthan Vatakketath Ravi

To write a poem
Without me and you
And Neriamangalam,
I Reached
A seashore far away
And sat on the sand spread.
The salt brims over me
And the giddiness in the woods
Turns to waves.
When sat looking at the sea
Saw the lands abroad.
There saw the people
Working in the offices and factories
Sleeping and playing—
The people with various colours
And emotions.
I wished to drink
Their laughter And fondle
The sorrows there keeping them beside.

All of them
Gathered around in-dash
Love turned up as gentle winds
And blew the wings.
The dusk on the seashore Reddened more.

Laughter and shouts
And screams
Flown up as if songs.
And those who follow them and dance

And who are more depressed,
Sat together.
As a single continent,
Seashore
With everything becomes one world.

Like a ball the Earth
Started spinning itself underfoot.
With the speed of moving the leg
Earth is rotating on its own.
It is my legs spin
The Earth moving around the sun

Ha... Again
I unnecessarily have entered the poem
Haughtily.

All of them
Might have gone
To their own spaces.
With none, the sea
Turning blue,
Started playing making ripples.

How can I avoid me,
Searching my home
Bending
On the Earth?
Placing Neriyamangalam
On my lap
And nibble the poem.

Neriamangalam: Poet's homeland

The Beginning of the World

Translated by Dr. Sambhu R.

When you left
I felt silence transforming into a country
Clock hands turned to the moment
When the earth took birth
History began to write itself anew
The first signs of life came
Flicking their tails out of water
Dinosaurs roamed the earth
World Wars cried raucously for blood
Reddened by revolutions
Flags fluttered high in the air
Pele kicked the ball across the sky
Maradona punched it slyly into the net
And Higuita stood alone guarding the goalpost
Sachin brandished his bat triumphantly
Films and other artistic pursuits took centre stage
And we stopped talking...

When we reach this point in time,
How many times will the world have lost?

Our quarrel was not about nations
Vanishing from the globe
Or about economic policies or transactions

We were subjecting to chemical change
Those inner agonies of the soul
That nobody would understand

And since someone might discover them
And set them down
As love's fourth law of motion

Let us now cement the silence between us
With stricter equations
Do not make any noise
If we do, we might start to cry
With far greater innocence
Than the first-ever life form

In the beginning, there was not the Word
Instead, there was Angst.

In The Dusk of Swirling Sounds

Translated by Haris Yoonus

Amid the roaring cheers
I spun the DJ mixer
Created new shades of music
Swinging my chair
Painting fresh waves of sounds.

Filmmakers, authors and
Artists ceased to listen
A few danced
Running amidst
Unnamed trees
Drenched of pale sunlight
Leaves drooped as notes
Having no address
Nor direction
Amongst the benches
In a terrible and vibrant enthuse...

At times, the rain became songs,
Unheard ragas blooming anew
Assorted men, women and children
As old as me
Yet bearing no mass of age

Drank, swayed and ate
Sprouting fresh paths of colour

Eyes full of romance
Ears full of music
Words full of love

The hills afar moved closer
Pulling nearby trees along

Kites hung on the clouds
Hovered away
While children crafted
Wide range of kites eternally

What flowed through the river,
If not me, I knew it wasn't you either.
So close it was,
That slope untouched by darkness.

Flat winds brushed against fingers,
Taking flight as new verses.

Though a cup full of silence
Was poured aside,
I had no craving to be soaked within,
In this twilight
Nestled between sea and the woods.

Before someone unravels
The little of me that remained,
They walked along,
Each to their long path.

Sounds echoing with deep colours,
Sat in tied-up chairs.

Painting scentless flowers in the
Vast canvas
The circles expanding

To burn as bright as the sun

How ample are the sights
This evening nap brings...
Everything must be scraped off
Before I wake

Better than the day
Is this very darkness
Spinning out from the DJ mixer!

Coffee Time

Translated by Arun T. Vijayan

The moments
That were lost between us
Came to my bedside
With the laziness of slumber
In the early morning.

I offered a glass of rain
To start the conversation,
But she wanted warmth.
After having something sweet,
She continued staring at the corner of the room.

Then, right at that very moment!

Like balloons in the hands,
The white clouds walk along the old paths.

When the fingers touched the trees,
Colours that had never existed before
Bloomed and blossomed,
And the hands glowed!
Suddenly, the wings unfolded.

We flew with the birds,
Tossing the warmth,
We had scooped out to each other.

You feel cold even when it's warm.
The breeze lingers on your fingers,
And now we are kites at the edge of the wind.

Who is at the edge of that kite?
When we reached above the sea,
You stood close,
Joined your hand with mine,
Without fear of the depths below.

As we glided above
The distant houses, gardens, and farms,
Your fingers slowly slipped away.

I have leaped away from myself
With a sense of detachment.

Sleep rose
Louder than the sun.

Look! The rain
Offers me
A cup of sunlight.

Forest Climb

Translated by Dr. Jaya Anitha Abraham

I gave my body to her,
Entered the forest,
Scattering dry leaves—
The forest took me in.

The wild creepers
Pulled me nearer,
Getonia vines dripping sap
Green fingers tracing my skin.
The forest pressed its lips
Below my ear
From my face, chest, shoulders and legs,
Young shoots sprouted
In the whistling breeze.

Terminalia, Senna, Grevia
And many other forest trees
Embraced me playfully
With their leaves.

Wild jasmines brushed
The tip of my nose,
While a naked white pine stood near,
With its green-tinted love.
The mahogany laid a bed of leaves,
And wild magnolias cast their blooms.
The forest poured its longing into me
As I lay stretched on my back.

The loins of the boulders grew moist,

Birds twittered with joy,
Bursting into squeals of delight
And fell silent.

The forest laid its head
And rested on my chest,
As the sky kept silent watch.

The Gliricidia Flowers

Translated by Arun T. Vijayan

You died on the day
When Gliricidia bloomed in clusters,
Its branches reaching out,
As you slipped away, submerged in the river.
Amid the murmurs of the crowd,
I watched the whirlpool in the river's heart
Pull you under,
And wished to sink away too.
No matter how deep I dive,
The River will carry me back, tangled in its embrace.
Since you sank beneath the waters,
I've longed to carve a path down,
To reach you.
It's been a long time now,
Since I drifted away from you.
On the night you left,
When I placed Gliricidia flowers
Upon your grave,
You smiled.
No grave could ever bury
The warmth of your smile.
As I stood gazing
At the earth soaked in fallen candles,
The dead rose up, one by one.
Like lilies in bloom,
They all stood in a circle,
You and I at the center,
Dancing to the song:
"Maranam Varumoru Naal
Orkkuka Marthya Nee,"*

On the borders of the graveyard,
Gliricidia bloomed in full.
On that same night, I swam and
Reached the whirlpool where you sank.
Diving into the depths,
Without flowing into the abyss,
Your smile blooms, untouched, and remains.
The Gliricidia flowers formed a spring
Even in the river's depth.
How did you,
Who swam and defeated
Both me and the flow,
Touch the depths?
In anger, I kicked the river
With my foot.
The river churned once,
And the whirlpool grew larger.
From the depths,
You stretched out your hand and called...
How can I turn away from you,
With the face of Mother Mary?
I walked towards the depths
To touch your hands.
Instead of water in the river,
Gentle violet flowers flowed.

---

*Malayalam funeral song which meaning 'Death will come one day, remember, O man'

Akbarovsky

Translated by Arun T. Vijayan

As I walk along with
Dmitri, Ivan, and Alyosha-
The sons of Karamazov-
Through Russian streets,
You should come toward us,
Hat tipped low from afar.
The moment we saw you,
We fluttered, stirred;
My mind flooded with frenzy,
Sinking into delirium...
And you, you must smile now.
As laughter sears through the mind,
We stand-four of us,
Only four-
We'll turn the street into a garden of flowers,
And in the frost of madness,
Fall, naked and wild, with a cry.
After so many years,
You'll see me walk
That same Russian street...
Through the sting of vodka
Seeking your lost smile.
I'll bite the frayed edges
Of a cigar's frenzied thoughts.
Not now...
But after a long, long time.
Fyodor... dear father of time...
May I touch your beard
With her laughter...

Then let the light of delirium
Spill forth like a radiant dawn.
Your name is not Anna...
Alyosha, Dmitri, Ivan...
Calling out louder and louder...
Yet in this wintry chill,
In the light that never fades,
In the warmth of the cigar,
Through the sharp sting of vodka,
Will you call me Akbarovsky?
Will you laugh again,
Just laugh, without any reason?

The Wound

Translated by Arun T Vijayan

Within a healed wound
Another wound may-
Still lie awake.
Each season
Leaves a mark
Upon memory.
They'll bloom into laughter,
Sweat beads glistening in the sun,
Walking along with the rain.
A wound holds
Its own quiet thoughts.
When I ask if it has healed,
The inner wound awakens,
Stirring in pain.
Sometimes,
It lies still-
Just skin,
As if lifeless.
It isn't the unhealed wound,
But the wound that has dried deeper
That startles me.
In this body called "me,"
How much dread does a wound hold
When it arrives without flesh?
Within the inner wound
Some poems lie torn,
Waiting to emerge
Whenever it desires.

A wound isn't always that simple-
Especially when the inner wound
Bears no resemblance to the one outside.

Time Is Not a Temporal Art

Translated by Sajai K.V.

A girl walks with a guitar on her shoulder
The guitar lay mum within the bag with
Subdued anger
Abruptly
A bird alights on the bag
The girl, scared, throws the bag
To the ground
The bird pecks at the zip
And music spills over
The city among the hills
With the guitar singing
Birds came fluttering
Flowering trees sprouted
All over the hills
Flowers with various hues brought fragrance in profusion
Waterfalls bubbled blue
Even the girl was startled
To laughter and the
People too laughed
The city danced blissfully
Bees, birds and flies
Swarmed in the streets
Beasts came quietly walking
Mammoth mansions were lit up
Men, animals and little living things were afloat on a gust of music
The bird flew away from the bag
Music, suddenly, came to a close
Only the horns blared
The girl disappeared in the meanwhile

The bag lay agape
The guitar walked away
Alone and aimlessly
Again the mundane life in the city
Again the monotonous rain in the mountains
The guitar may be sitting and singing alone
Somewhere
Time, unlike music,
Doesn't linger anywhere...

Silent, Detached

Translated by Devi Priya

You
Moving between the trees
Like breeze

You
Watching yourself in the river
Like rain

Sunshine
Drying itself
Over the fields

Same breath
Same words
Same smell
We put out
All memories
The same day

Life is now
Silent like love
And detached
Like God

Rashes

Translated by Sheeba Dilshad

I gazed at the sky
Above the almond trees
And traced the face
Of Nabi.*
My mother called me close,
Saying, "One line is enough."
She sketched a moon,
The size of a pathiri,*
On my thigh
With a ginberry twig.
That thought still lingers,
Its echo scratching gently
Within me, even now...

---

*Nabi: Indicates Prophet Mohammad
*Pathiri: Rice Pancake made by Kerala Muslims

An Evening in Menaka Junction

Translated by Arun T. Vijayan

Some strangers glance and laugh at me
As I pause, weary,
Searching for someone
Among those drifting away
From Menaka Junction
In an evening.
So many colors, so many scents,
All of them empty,
Feelingless.
I wonder, in this crowd,
Does anyone remember me?
The hot rays
Walk unsteadily
Out from the bars,
Weeping and laughing,
Embracing the dusk,
With the red sun trailing along.
The street vendors—
Of dreams in every color call out,
"Whatever your hopes may be,
Come and choose your dreams-
All at a grand discount!"
Just nearby,
An old man has stacked
Bad dreams and waits for someone.
He sits in silence,
Without calling out anything.
The clusters of nightmares
May find their sleep in packets.

In their dreams,
Who might linger there?
Even those who crawl back from the bars,
In blackout,
Ignored him.
I walked along the lake's shore.
Boatmen, setting sail to heaven, call out-
"Whatever your faith may be,
We can guide you to peace in your heavens.
For those without belief,
Consider it as a time travel.
"Heaven is not meant to be dreamed;
It is meant to be lived,"
Reads the writing on the boat named Heaven.
Parudeesa, Firdaus, Devalokam*—
Each boat bears a name, each with its own charm.
The travelers queued in line,
Draped in robes of color.
The boat's guard lifted his head and announced,
"The boat to hell has departed."
As I returned to Menaka Junction,
A little girl was selling yellow flowers.
With a glance, she seemed to say,
"Take these, brother;
Just a breath of their scent will ease your sorrows."
Her innocent smile echoed,
As if assuring, "Yes, that's true."
The sun departed,
And dreams sparkled in the shops.
The one who sold nightmares
Was nowhere to be seen.
The flower girl said,
"That's my grandpa.

He can't sell flowers
That carry nightmares,
So he left."
I bought a yellow flower
And walked into the night.
The sellers of dreams called out loudly,
"Sir..."
I inhaled the flower's fragrance deeply,
Menaka Junction faded from my mind,
She had gifted me a pack of nightmares, secretly
I walked on, clutching it in my hand.
When my sorrows faded,
I turned off the screen of nightmares.
There, the yellow flowers bled on their petals,
Erasing sorrows one by one.
Nightmares glimmer in the darkness!

---

*Menaka: A street in Cochin.

*Parudeesa, Firdaus, Devalokam: Names meaning Paradise.

Letter to Theo

Translated by Binu Karunakaran

Seeing sunflowers
No more triggers Van
Gogh. Only
The glare is seen,
An yellow plastered
On to the light. Sun
And its shimmer
Remain unseen. Woman
Who arrives
Walking from a distance
Has the colour of sun-
Flower; If she
Smiles,
For certain I'll
Cry! You may
Adore works of Van
Gogh, they give
Me seizures. Who
Likes to see
The image of a boiling sun?
Cutting off an ear
Isn't sweet as me
Plucking a sunflower.
Set them afire
And see sunflowers
Fly off
Vincent's canvases.

Beyond the Bend

Translated by Arun T. Vijayan

Beyond the turning, you wait-
And that's why,
Songs I've never heard before
Sprout in the yard by the roadside,
Just beyond the bend.
Scorched, withered plants begin to green,
And from the dry earth,
A new rain-scent rises.
Beyond the turning, you wait-
Your smile, a kiss on my face
Carried by the breeze.
But I have never gone beyond the bend.
Even so, I see you there,
I hear you there.
Though unseen,
You are there.
I may never see you –
Yet I can hear
The chime of the crystal bangles you wear.
So why the need to see you at all?
On a morning filled with music,
I drifted far away.
Years later, when I return,
The bend is gone-
A four-lane road stretches ahead,
Its own momentum pushing forward,
Accelerating into the distance.
I stand in the yard,
Where have the songs and plants gone?
The bend has straightened,

And they may pass over your house.
How lonely a life without bends can be.
Somewhere along the long road,
There will be a bend,
And there you will be.
On the road without bends,
A sudden scream
Breaks the silence, and the brakes screech.
I prayed for the bends,
For you, whom I have never seen
Standing beyond them.
Songs and plants,
They don't just sprout in vain, do they?

A Prayer for Hell

Translated by Ra Sh

I walk through silence
Like a seed sprouting
Like the silence of a tomb.
Now, one can pray for the sun and
Claim no knowledge of the rain.

When sprawling without a possession,
Don't visit with flowers.
Only the kiss of the roots
Deeper than the darkness suffices.

Under the earth
I want to dream about
The hell that poetry is.

Wings of the Night

Translated by Arun T Vijayan

One draws this night as day,
Another as twilight,
Yet another as dawn.
In hues only their hearts know.

That is why
Each colour fades,
Disappearing from
The palette of dreams.

We can call this night
Not just night alone,
At times, it stretches forth
And can be called the day.

Otherwise,
There would be no wings
To circle endlessly
In the dance of light
Around the lamps.

Me

Translated by Binu Karunakaran

Tried lying supine
Spread like a road
No one walked.

Rose up tree-like
Into the sky
No one nested.

To flow like river
And row a boat
Who has time.

Poetry Studio

Translated by Achuthan Vatakketath Ravi

Kept the paper and pen aside
In respite.
Suddenly,
A lass appeared before me.
Won't you write a poem about me?

When I asked what her name was,
She answered:
I do not have a name.
The poem must be about me
That's all.

She flew away,
Rising.
When I took the paper
There was a poem
With the ink not gone dry
And also, a feather.

Self-Absorption

Translated by Arun T Vijayan

You unearthed the dream
I tucked within hidden leaves,
And laughed it into song:
"Stars, moonlight,
And the beauty of evening."

You uncovered the word
I hid within the lines of verse,
And wept, whispering:
"Silence, love,
And a poem."

You find yourself
Within my innermost depths,
Where I concealed you,
Whispering, "I am, I am."

Silence at a Crescendo

Translated by Ra Sh

There are some feminine dreams
Where only silence reigns.
One should rush in And rush off
After planting a kiss.

The lips and cheeks would bloom
Like flowers scented with
Sudden exclamations.

Isn't it at such a deep silence
That the world shrieks?

There are some feminine bodies
That get wet in silence.
One feels like sponging up
When no one is noticing
The beads of sweat
That laugh uproariously.

The limbs get interchanged and
Go mad in the brilliance of
The tastes and aromas.
One loves so much
The noisy memories
That are silent
At a distance.

Affection

Translated by Arun T Vijayan

When I prayed for the rain,
You clung to my heart
Like a drifting cloud.

When I yearned for dusk,
You unveiled the sun
That rested on your brow.

When you were touched
In your heart for me,
You slipped away from mine...

When I Love a Woman

Translated by Ra Sh

How do I love a woman?
Swaying her like the wind
On the sea shore
Or like the breeze that
Touches the leaves on the
River bank,
Drizzling on her, then storming,
Cloud bursting upon her
Or spattering like the sun's glare.?
Is it like the buds sprouting on
The wild trees or like the flowers
That touch the thorns in the courtyards
And laugh in the flow of fragrance?
How does one love?
Hiding it like a poem one reads alone
And torn to shreds later?
Screaming like a swarming city or
Walking lazily on the banks of the backwaters
At the end of an evening of songs?
Loving means
Vocalizing light, turning swaras
Into colours and painting abstractly.
Like the seed sprouting without
The earth's knowledge,
We can call it the harvest of silence or
The harmony of the thumping chest.
Not very simple is
Love in this world.

Bansuri

Translated by Dr. Sambhu R

Wavelets of melodious music
Ripple from the maestro's* bansuri,
Immersing me in a rapturous trance
As I stand in the moonlight
Watching the sky spread its canopy
Of stars over my head.
I can also hear the darbari* of screams
In the poem recited by the river.
In which sher* will I hide my wails
Addressed to you?
In which matla* will I offer you
My passionate avowals of love?
Moonlight comes flowing sinuously
Down the throat of a narrow alley.
The jasmines growing in my courtyard
Will have bloomed tonight;
The queen of the night
Might be closing its eyelids now
With a prayer to see the moon;
And all the paths will end endlessly.
Dawn shows me the way to your house
Through the rubber trees.
Bereft of your presence,
The house is as terrifying as the sound
Emanating from a severed tongue.
If I walk this way, I can reach you.
See, all the flowers have bloomed.
I want to keep gazing at your peacock eyes
Till morning and mumble you...you.
I want to tell you

While listening to the strains of a ghazal
Sung in charukeshi*
That I have no one but you
And that the mountains are thirsting
To see the rain come down.
I want to die and be born again
The same night,
And when the sun opens his fiery fist
In the east,
Follow in the footsteps of death
With an aching heart.
Death is the answer, life the question.
But...
The maestro's bansuri
Keeps on raining music...

---

*The maestro referred to here is Hariprasad Chaurasia
*Darbari – a Hindustani raga
*Sher – a ghazal couplet
*Matla – the first couplet of a ghazal
*Charukeshi – a Hindustani raga

The Day of the Kisses

Translated by Ra Sh

One morning,
Or earlier than the mornings,
The ummas* in Kuzhur Wilson's* poems
Pressed my calling bell.
When the doors did not open,
Lips began to knock at the doors.
When the doors were opened
The kisses rushed in and
Roamed around all the rooms.
Not finding my Umma**, they
Fell very sad.
One of the kitten watching
Pawed the kisses.
Wrestling with kitten,
The kisses began to play.
The cat eyes shone in the light.
In the light of the cat eyes
The leaves of the courtyard plants
Turned a dark shade of green.
The vehicles speeding on the highway
Began to slow down and flow with the breeze.
In the room that Umma used to lie down,
In the palm marks on the wells
When she balanced herself to walk,
Everywhere the kisses rushed around
Enthusiastically.
The entire Neryamangalam
Was chockfull of kisses.

The river flowed with the fluttering fish.
The elephants and the rabbits in the jungle
Became calm with the kisses.
The birds sang paeans of the kisses.
The silence that reigned till then
Gave way to many kinds of songs.
The screams turned into
The joy of many pleasant moments.
Under the dancing steps,
Flowers blossomed.
In any case, how can one write down
Love without kisses?

---

*Kuzhur Wilson is a famour Malayali poet
*Umma – kiss.
**Umma – mother.

Byline*

Translated by Dr. Sambhu R.

When ambulances grind
To a halt in the driveway
Of the hospital, the mind
Performs a headcount
Of those brought in dead—
One, two, three, four, it counts
Till with each death ticked off
On fingers, grief defers
Its pursuit for a vent!—
What if more ambulances
Arrive with their dead?
My heart swoons with joy
At the prospect of a news column
Bearing my name as its byline*
Gracing tomorrow's front page.
Just as thoughts of fame fill
My journalistic mind
And visions of fecundity
Start to titillate, I see
My little daughter's corpse
Brought in, white flowers
Gleaming in her nostrils.
I call out to the heavens,
Pointing an accusatory finger,
And hurry after her,
Casting away my damned pen.
I start counting again—
One, two, three, four...
Thinking the game of hide-and-seek
She is playing with life will end

Any minute now,
But still she lies eyes shut
In the mortuary's final darkness.

---

*Byline refers to the line at the head of a newspaper article carrying the writer's name.

Antonyms

Translated by Sheeba Dilshad

In the valley of deep sorrow,
Some houses stood
With names like
Agony, Melancholy, or Lament.
Every day, they cook sorrow there;
You can see a heavy flow of
Desolation even in their laughter.
They clean their courtyard in sorrow,
Plant thorny shrubs of agony,
Crying out alongside love.
Sadness splutters within desire,
And not a single leaf remains there
Without bowing its head.
On weekends, they gather together
In rooms of sorrow and sit in silence.
Even the candles burn down in weep,
With endless songs of lament.
The seeds they plant bear fruit
Without ever blossoming.
Their games, their laughter—
Everything is steeped in grief.
In the pleasures of evening,
You can see the children
Endlessly spinning sorrow.
When the kites of gloom
Fly high in the valleys,
We, the people
Who dwell in houses
Named Happiness, Pleasure,

Or Cheerfulness, live
On the other side of the mountains.
We dance with utmost contentment,
Afraid that our joy may be overheard
By those beyond the mountains.
Ignoring this fear, we celebrate
Each and every moment,
But their mourning sounds
Rise louder and louder,
Above all.
The gale howls through their gardens,
Their houses fly away.
The slates where they wrote sorrows
Burst apart and fall
Into our courtyards.
Naming them milkweeds and butterflies,
The children and adults
Chase after them.
We are trying to step ahead,
With screams as the background.
You can move backward,
But before that,
There's a chance to bind you
With despair,
Only to burst into laughter.
Yes, it is not far away.
So many know—
Sorrow is not
Even the antonym of happiness!
Yes, it is not far away
Who knows
Sorrow is not the antonym
Of happiness!

The Goalie is Not So Lonely

Translated by Dr. Sambhu R.

Should the goalie be so lonely?
I think not.
And there is a reason for thinking so.
Long back,
Whenever I put on the garb
Of the goalie,
I never once felt lonely.
The ball would come bouncing
Evasively towards me
As though the whole wide world
Was rushing into the net.
At the same time,
Images of players aiming the ball
At the dead centre of the net
On every soccer field on earth
All at once
Would swirl as in a kaleidoscope
Before my eyes.
Whenever I leapt to grab the ball,
I would remember the poor, poor earth.
Afraid that someone might kick
The ball out of my hands,
I would start tackling imaginary foes.
Once someone dribbled the ball forward,
Trying to sneak it past my defence.
I stretched my hands wide open
Not knowing what to do,
And guess what got caught in my hands—
It was the earth!

A scorpion kick,
And the court went crazy!
I punted solitude far, far away
Just like that...
Oh, it landed in the opposite goalpost
Amidst exuberant shouts of "Goal"!

House

Translated by Dr. Sambhu R.

My house embodies
The right of rain
And golden sunshine
To occupy it
Without the least thought
That it is mine.

My house for me
Is a roofless dream,
A conch echoing
An innocent scream.

My house is the charity
Of the spate that resolves
The raging dispute
Between one side
Of my mind which says
I am the house
And the other which says,
No, it is you.

Now my house is the rain,
The noonday haze,
The forest, poesy-
Its meanings continue
Forever to multiply.

I have no walls
Except what the wind
In its infinite mercy

Erects for me.
I am born of the sky;
I have no roof
Over my head
Or floor under my feet.

Lonely World... Come, Let's Draw Dali's Moustache

Translated by Dr. Sambhu R.

In the obscure corner of a town
Deserted by all its inhabitants,
In that final dissolving emptiness
In which not a trace of me is left,
A yellow flower lying prostrate
Teaches the alphabet of love,
Winding its arms
Around the wind's waist,
And then everything starts to melt
As in Dali's famous painting.
Why else is the town
Bereft of its people now?
Paths where men and women
Used to walk abreast
Waving their arms about;
Places where they milled around
To buy vegetables and fish.
That night of savouring drugs
When crystal glasses
Plunged into the frothy ferment
Of impetuous thoughts
For transient bliss
And mattresses were overturned
By the overspill of blood-spattered love.
Then midnights that took off their underclothes.
Oh! Without reminiscence or oblivion
The town starts trudging alone through me.
Myriad scents
Kisses
Deep comings and goings.

How many are the faces that wiped clean
The body when it broke into sweat?
Do you remember those streets
That are not the least unfamiliar,
Streets that are not at all distant
Or dimming in sight?
I had stopped telling my story
Before the yellow flower wilted,
And then I transformed into you...
Dali's moustache brushed against my cheek.
Beneath the poem
A city takes off its underskirt.
Someone is erasing a painting...

Wahyu*

Translated by Sheeba Dilshad

The angels visit not only
The Prophets
But me also!
A man with dazzling
Light came
In the first day
Though there was
Light,
He flew to me
With cool wings
That
I can't believe
At first!
When he asked me
In the feeble voice
Of snow
To read
I trembled with fear
Zammiluni*
I cried aloud,
She held me
Tight using
An old cloth
Another angel
Transformed cold
Into warmth
While sleeping
He came from
Torrid
Fire mountains

He also said
"Read"
How can I read
Even without
A single book
'Please give me
A newspaper
At least....'
She uttered something
And slept again.
When I woke up
And opened the door
See,
Another one stood there!
For my luck
He didn't ask me
To read
Instead he just touched
In my throat
From the day after
Nobody thinks about
Me at all
I walked through
The burning
Incense sticks
That has
Any fragrance
At all..
What to say to you
About 'the Wahyu'
I got!

---

* Wahyu: Revelation, *Zammiluni: Hold me tight

Grief

Translated by Dr. Sambhu R.

There is the dark green forest
And with it the river arrested in its flow
The diminutive moon I sketched long ago
In my infancy has not grown yet
There are also creeping plants
With flowers bursting from their roots
Caught in the rain, the sunshine shivers
All paths fork back to where they began
A page blanched by the absence
Of poetry and love lies faceup
Woes that are yet far away
Don't you silence me thus...
Is there anything more pious than grief?

Monsoons

Translated by Sheeba Dilshad

I called the first rain of Summer
With your name.
When the raindrops kisses the earth,
I remember your aroma.
Each first rain
Resembles first love,
A dream that increases
Your heart beat.
The summer offers
A white paper
To write about
The flowers that I forgot
To offer you.
Your name like rain
Filled all the pages.
What can I say about
The subconscious
Liquidity's bitter words?
To whom I talk
About raindrops?
The mountains sing
In the voice of breeze,
The sky,
A vast desert of silence...
And here—
A drop of rain
Falls from above,
From you to me.
I
Forgot you..!

Stay Still

Translated by Priya Unnikrishnan

Tired legs of constant walking
Froze suddenly in a day.
It didn't move a little.
Even the legs tried hard.
That's how shoes are made.

Where Laughter Originates from

Translated by Dr. Sambhu R.

Once cries hovered around in the wind
That rushed down from the mountains.
From which unknown land
Beyond the mountains
Could the cries have come
Fluttering high in the air like butterflies?

I remembered the houses there;
Then I saw the frightened eyes inside them.
Perhaps, the cries came
Fluttering from the din
Of the houses being pulled down.
But no one had ears for them!

Now they burrow into my ears,
Hurting my hearing.

I told the children that there exist
Trees that bear cries
Beyond the mountains
From where rain and sunshine arrive.
How they laughed hearing that!
Oh, I should have known that cries
Are not so innocent as laughter!

On this side of the houses of cries,
On this side of the mountains and trees,
In the room inside my house,
In the room inside my room,

I start laughing
And all my cries turn to laughter!

Lone

Translated by Priya Unnikrishnan

In In this hard loneliness
Will you remember me
Even from a distant point?

The memories of
Hate, love and lust.

In this loneliness, I can feel
Someone walking on the roads,
Saying something,
And being anxious
About the missing phone call,
A bunch of flowers blooming
From deep melancholy
And spreads its fragrance
Throughout my frenzy

A woodland path
Creeping through the green,
A lonely tree will blossom
Far away in the city,
My severe depression
Spin into mad by love
And sleep in its Profundity

So, when alone
Surprise me with your presence,
Being alone is not easy.

Spring in the Cemetery

Translated by Sajai K.V.

It is the memories of the dead
That blooms in the cemetery.

I put my ears close to the wall
To hear memories blooming .

The diurnal wreath
Of sunshine ,
The sighing of
Church bells
And the congregations.

Sight and wind.
How can we hear
the memories of the dead?

The nocturnal cemetery
Whispers of spring
Making me shudder with
Fear.

Lo, the cross
is blossoming !

Pencil Memory

Translated by Arun T. Vijayan

I bought a rubber,
To erase the memory of—
Those who remember,
But when the erasing began,
The pencil's tip broke off.

It wasn't anyone who broke it—
It was the pencil itself,
Remembering.

Sleep

Translated by Sajai K.V.

Night
The road lights darkness.

You, from afar,
Puts out sleep.

I make the bed
In poetry.

Still time to close
The eyes.

The Snow Cross of December

Translated by Dr. Jaya Anitha Abraham

In the night
The snow whispers
Your name
The village reminisces about, you
Babies drift into dreams
And smile.

You cry
Beside me, you sit
Wiping your cheeks
With a handkerchief and so on

Turning the pages
Of the new calendar
The sun-kissed children
Look for the birth sign
Of the rain.
They do not know
That the rain
Slipped away
Following you.

I kneel
Before your image
With silent prayers
Spun from long meditations
Oh, rain
Why do you not see me?

December blooms
In tiny flowers
Across the cemetery,
A crown of snow-thorns
Sits on my village's head
Oh, Mary
Why did you weep?
Behind the glass-case of snow?

When will she come again?
All day long
She hurried, made the manger
Hung the stars
Soaked in the hailstorm
Of the night
She stayed awake
And teased,
That lilies bloom
In my heart
And that I carry
An olive-green shadow.

December,
Return her to me
These nights,
Let me melt like candles
Before the graveyard
Let me kneel down
Every Sunday
To pray for rain.
And at the end
When summer comes
With its poems

Let me plead: 'Go away, go away'.
Let us cry out
To the moonlight
That we may pray
To fast the whole day
And break the fast in the evening
When we see her
December,
Return her to me.

Watching you,
The breeze hides
Among the young leaves
Of the bamboo bush.

Waiting for you
The streams cease their flow
In search of you
The plants fill the courtyard
With their buds.

December,
We deserve tears
Let me nail my palm
Against your snow.

Chothi Papaan

Translated by Arun T. Vijayan

He always walked –
With the forest.
When he arrived,
The forest followed,
The rustle of leaves
Accompanying him.
Once, he suddenly passed away,
And on that day,
The forest must have cried.
The water in the river
Had risen high.

Chothi Papaan: A Malayalam Traditional name.

We Are in the Same Bus

Translated by Achuthan Vatakketath Ravi

I know
We are in the same bus
Dashing afar.
I and you are travelling
Without seeing each other.

Along with the songs
Your fingers are beating rhythm
On some seats
The winds of it
Turn my fingers
To the strings of guitar.

It makes me sad that
You are not knowing,
When the driver stretches the bends
You bend to right
And the leaves outside
Touch on your face.
You do not know it
You are flying

On the songs.
When does the bus stop?
I am the only traveler
In this fast – running bus
Which has no stop at all.
The driver and others vanish
Only I do not see you.
When the melancholy rises

You may be weeping.

It touches me as rain.

Even after the bell rang*
The bus runs swiftly
Then
Where
When
And how do we get down?
The bus is a world.

---

*To stop a running bus the conductor rings a single bell and to start again, two bells.

Livelihood

Translated by Arun T. Vijayan

Why fear a caterpillar,
Turning green while feeding
On chlorophyll beneath the leaves?

It simply fulfils its role,
Dutifully consuming its share.
Yet, none punish us
We, who devour the same leave.

When the Bamboos Sing

Translated by K.C. Muraleedharan

When, in the hall, drenched in qawwali,
The concertgoers, their fingers dancing,
Far off, in a hamlet,
A boy was busy
Making a bamboo flute.

When the first hole he makes
Raag pahadi gently flows
With the red-hot compass
boring the second hole
Megh-malhar effuses.

The qawwali rains on
The listeners float on its surges

From his flute unique
Ragas rise unbidden
When he drives holes
With his dusky fingers and red-hot compass
Far-off here, in the room air-cooled
The bansuri goes dumb.

The boy's bamboo flute
Plays bright and hard
into the qawwali's infinite charms.
They in the hall writhed
As if the hot compass pricked.
The rain subsides
And the Sun rises scorching
Like the red-hot compass tip.

The hall abounds with melting ragas
The world
Starts speaking in sharp notes and nuances
Basant Mukhari overflows
Tears stream down
The hall, all rains.

On his lips
The Baul dances
Bamboos sing in the chorus.

About the Translators

Ra Sh (Ravi Shanker N.) is a poet and translator based in Palakkad, Kerala. He has published four collections of poetry: *Architecture of Flesh* (Poetrywala), *Bullet Train and Other Loaded Poems* (Hawakal), *Kintsugi by Hadni* (RLFPA), and *Buddha and Biryani* (Hawakal), along with a chapbook, *In the Mirror, Our Graves*, co-authored with Ritamvara Bhattacharya. He has also published a play, *Blind Men Write* (Rubric Publishing).

As a translator, his English translations include *Mother Forest* (Women Unlimited), *Waking is Another Dream* (Navayana), *Don't Want Caste* (Navayana), *Kochiites* (Greenex), *How to Translate an Earthworm* (Dhauli Books), and *The Ichi Tree Monkey and New and Selected Stories of Bama* (Speaking Tiger).

Achuthan Vatakketath Ravi is a retired Headmaster of Parudur High School in Pattambi, Kerala. A poet, writer, and literary critic, he entered the world of poetry in 1975 with the translation of Khalil Gibran's *Countryman*. His first published story was a translation of *Wanka* by Anton Chekhov, which appeared in the children's magazine *Thatthmma*. He has also published translations of Pashtun poetry and Russian poetry in *Malayalantu* and *Navamalayali* (online magazines), respectively. He took part in the International Poetry Meet – Prime Poetry Festival and Prize – on March 10, 2019, and published his first poem, *Locusts*, in the collection. He also participated in an International Poetry Meet conducted at Govt. Printing Technology, Perintalmanna (online), and published a poem, *Divorce*, in the collection *Rhyming Nature*, released in connection with the International Poetry Meet in December 2021.

Inquisitive, passionate, and restless like a child, he shows us how to remain monstrously creative even at the age of seventy.

Sajay K. V. is a renowned literary critic in Malayalam, regularly contributing insightful columns to prominent magazines. His critiques have earned recognition in literary circles. His notable works, such as *Cleopatrayodoppam Oru Rathri* (translation), *Shari: Pavayoyival*, and *Kadalas Marikkayilla: Chavarayachan*, reflect his deep engagement with literature and contemporary issues.

Binu Karunakaran is a poet, translator, and journalist based in Kochi, Kerala. A winner of the Charles Wallace India Trust Fellowship, his portfolio of poems, *Muchiri*, was commended by the Michael Marks Awards for Poetry Pamphlets 2021, judged by a panel headed by Ruth Padel.

Dr. Jaya Anitha Abraham was born in the Pathanamthitta district and has been teaching at Abu Dhabi University since 2011. She is also a Fellow of the Academy of Higher Education. Her published works include *When the Walls Have Ears*, a translation of the Malayalam novel *Nilachoru* by Shabu Kilithattil. She writes poetry in Malayalam and English and translates literary works from Malayalam into English. In her poems, her inner self merges with nature and the world around her.

Arun T. Vijayan is a Malayalam poet and media personality. He was born and raised in Thiruvankulam, Ernakulam District, Kerala. He has published various poems in Malayalam periodicals. Two of his translated works—*Lokathilettavum Santhoshavanaya Manushyan* (a translation of Eddie Jaku's life story, *The Happiest Man on Earth*, published by Manjul Publications) and *Thirayoli* (a translation of Kalkki Krishnamoorthy's novel *Alai Osai*, published by Pappathi Pusthakangal)—have also been published.

Poet and Translator **Devipriya** writes in English and Malayalam. Her poems have been published in print media like *Mathrubhumi* and in online media. She was awarded the third prize in the prestigious International English Poetry Writing Competition held by Poesis Online & Xpress Publications.

Priya Unnikrishnan is a bilingual writer residing in Texas, USA. Her poems have been published in many international magazines.

Dr. Sambhu R. hails from Kayamkulam, a small town in the district of Alappuzha, Kerala. He writes in both English and Malayalam. He is employed as an Assistant Professor of English at N.S.S. College, Pandalam. *Vavval Manushyanum Komaliyum*, published by Pappathi Pusthakangal in 2019, was his first book of poems in Malayalam. His poems in English have appeared in *Wild Court, Bombay Literary Journal, Muse India, Borderless Journal, Setu,* and *Shot Glass Journal*, among others.

A native of Alappuzha, **Haris Yoonus** has been working in Dubai for the past 20 years. He has published three Malayalam poetry collections—*Puzhavith, Kadal Oru Galaxy,* and *Veyil Way Station*—through Kairali Books, which were released at the Sharjah International Book Fair in 2021, 2022, and 2024. He penned the lyrics for the lyrical video *Sugandhakalam*, composed by Bijibal and sung by Sudeep Kumar, which was released during Onam 2023. He regularly writes for periodicals, online magazines, and new media platforms.

Sheeba Dilshad is a multilingual poet and translator who writes in both Malayalam and English. Her first anthology, *Avasanathe Akashavum Pakshikalum*, was published in 2020 by Logos Publications, Pattambi. She now writes poems for leading Malayalam periodicals.

K. C. Muraleedharan is an associate professor of English who retired from Payyanur College, Kannur University. He served as the principal of St. Joseph's College, Pilathara, for five years. His contributions in English include the translation of the first draft of Pattom Thanu Pillai's biography published in 2012, translated and co-translated poems from Malayalam to English published in Countercurrents.org, Malayalam Literary Survey, www.modernpoetry.org besides seven edited collections of prose, poetry and essays for undergraduates of various universities. He co-edited with E. V. Ramakrishnan the book O. V. Vijayan: The Critical Insider, a Routledge, London publication, 2025.